North Suburban Library District
Loves Park, ILL.

All injuries to books beyond reasonable wear and all losses shall be made good to the satisfaction of the Librarian.

Each borrower is held responsible for all books drawn on his card and for all fines accruing on the same.

PLEASE NOTIFY US IF YOUR
LIBRARY CARD IS LOST OR STOLEN

HOW THE US SECURITY AGENCIES WORK

by Allan B. Cobb

UNITED STATES OF AMERICA

Content Consultant
Dr. Lamont Colucci
Chairman, Politics Department
Coordinator, National Security Studies Program
Ripon College

Core Library

An Imprint of Abdo Publishing
www.abdopublishing.com

www.abdopublishing.com

Published by Abdo Publishing, a division of ABDO, PO Box 398166, Minneapolis, Minnesota, 55439. Copyright © 2015 by Abdo Consulting Group, Inc. International copyrights reserved in all countries. No part of this book may be reproduced in any form without written permission from the publisher. Core Library™ is a trademark and logo of Abdo Publishing.

Printed in the United States of America, North Mankato, Minnesota
092014
012015

Cover Photo: Charles Dharapak/AP Images
Interior Photos: Charles Dharapak/AP Images, 1; AP Images, 4, 10, 20, 28, 36, 40; National Security Agency, 6; Marcio Jose Sanchez/AP Images, 8, 45; Kirsty Wigglesworth/AP Images, 12; Library of Congress, 14, 16, 32; iStockphoto, 23; Shutterstock Images, 25; Bebeto Matthews/AP Images, 34; Susan Walsh/AP Images, 45

Editor: Heather C. Hudak
Series Designer: Becky Daum

Library of Congress Control Number: 2014944234

Cataloging-in-Publication Data
Cobb, Allan B.
 How the US Security agencies work / Allan B. Cobb.
   p. cm. -- (How the US government works)
ISBN 978-1-62403-638-5 (lib. bdg.)
Includes bibliographical references and index.
1. United States. National Security Agency/Central Security Service--Juvenile literature. 2. National Security--United States--Juvenile literature.
3. United States--Politics and government--Juvenile literature.   I. Title.
327--dc23
                                                    2014944234

CONTENTS

CHAPTER ONE

The Need for National Security

On June 5, 2013, a British newspaper printed an amazing story. The newspaper said the National Security Agency (NSA) had a secret court order. This order gave the NSA, an agency whose job is to monitor foreign nations' communications for national security purposes, the right to collect the phone records of millions of Americans. Each record tells who was contacted

People around the world held events in support of Edward Snowden. The former national intelligence worker broke the news about the NSA's secret court order to collect phone records.

The NSA headquarters are in Fort Meade, Maryland.

and when. Some records even show where a call was made. These records help the NSA paint a clear picture of suspects' communications. The news story also said the NSA wanted to collect the records of people who had not done anything wrong. Intelligence worker Edward Snowden had leaked these details to the press.

More details came out over the next few months. The three-month court order was one of many the NSA had been granted over the past three years. The

NSA said the records helped prevent terrorist attacks in the United States and around the world.

Many people were angry. They thought the government was spying on them. The government argued it was trying to protect US citizens. This job is done by many different groups. They include intelligence agencies, security agencies, and law enforcement agencies. Each group plays a different role in protecting the United States and its citizens.

The NSA is an intelligence agency. Its job is to protect the country from possible threats. Some people want to hurt the United States and its citizens. Part of the NSA's job is to find out about attacks before they happen. The agency tracks communication over the Internet and other systems to gather intelligence, or information. It then passes the information to other government agencies. The Central Intelligence Agency (CIA) is an example of another intelligence agency.

There were nearly 70 million international arrivals in the United States in 2013. Approximately 38 million came from Canada or Mexico.

Protecting Our Borders

Collecting data is just one way the government provides protection. Security agencies help protect our borders from possible threats. For example, people must pass through customs when they arrive on a flight from another country. Customs is a type of checkpoint. People show their passport to an agent before they enter the United States. The agent asks the person questions about why he or she is entering the United States. People who seem to be telling the truth are allowed onto US soil. Those who seem like they have something to hide go through more checks. For example, customs agents may check the person's bags for illegal items, such as drugs or weapons.

Customs is part of the Department of Homeland Security (DHS). The DHS was created in 2002. The DHS's job is to protect US borders and citizens from harm. Stopping illegal drugs from being brought into the country is part of

US Borders

The US Customs and Border Protection agency watches about 330 ports of entry and border crossings into the United States. These entry points include airports, seaports, and land crossings. Agents patrol the US borders with Mexico and Canada. In some places, agents patrol on foot. In other places, they travel by truck, plane, helicopter, or horse. Agents work day and night in all weather conditions. Their main goal is to prevent terrorists, drugs, and non-US citizens from illegally entering the United States.

Today there are more than 100 million fingerprints in security agency databases.

its job. The department also works to stop terrorism in the United States.

Investigations

Security agencies also help solve crimes. They work on criminal cases that impact the entire country. One of these agencies is the Federal Bureau of Investigation (FBI).

The FBI investigates crimes and enforces the law. Its job is to protect the United States and its people from threats such as terrorist attacks, crimes, fraud, and other illegal activities. The FBI has agents who work in the field to solve crimes. Some agents work undercover. Others use computers to find criminals. Some agents help state and local police. They provide access to databases that may help an investigation. Fingerprint records are an example of the data they provide.

Intelligence agencies, security agencies, and law enforcement agencies each play a role in protecting the United States. They work together to help make the United States more secure.

Fingerprint Database

Fingerprints are important clues. Security agencies began collecting fingerprint records in 1924. Prints left at the scene of a crime can be matched to fingerprints in the FBI database. This helps agents find out who committed the crime. Computers can match fingerprints to a suspect in less than two hours.

CHAPTER TWO

Intelligence Agencies

Intelligence is data that can be useful for making decisions. Most government agencies collect and analyze some type of data. Intelligence agencies focus on data about national security and possible threats. This data is shared with other agencies that work to protect the United States.

The CIA uses robotic aircraft to collect intelligence overseas.

Harry S. Truman was the thirty-third president of the United States. He served in this role from 1945 to 1953.

The Central Intelligence Agency

In 1942 President Franklin D. Roosevelt formed the Office of Strategic Services (OSS). The OSS collected and analyzed data to help the United States during World War II (1939–1945). After the war, the OSS was closed. Its intelligence duties were given to other departments.

President Harry S. Truman passed the National Security Act in 1947. The act formed the CIA and the National Security Council. The CIA's mission is to discover and stop threats to national security. It picked up the intelligence duties that had previously been done by the OSS.

The National Security Council advises the president on domestic, foreign, and military policies. It also ensures cooperation between military and intelligence agencies.

Gathering and Analyzing Data

Most CIA analysts gather and organize data. They gather data from the Internet, newspapers, magazines, and radio and TV programs from around the world. These sources provide clues about the current affairs of foreign countries. Some analysts use the data to draw conclusions and write reports about issues important to the United States. These reports are used by the president, Congress, and the military when passing laws or taking action on issues.

Satellite images also provide information about other countries. They show construction projects,

The CIA headquarters are located in Langley, Virginia.

numbers of planes and ships, locations of troops, and other useful details.

In some cases, the CIA uses spies to secretly collect data. This is done only by order of the president. In other cases, analysts decode secret messages they get from other countries' governments.

Once all types of information are combined, analysts try to make sense of the data. Their analyses help the CIA understand what is happening in other countries and how it could affect the United States.

The National Security Agency

During World War II, the US government learned the meanings of secret codes used by German and Japanese troops. The coded messages carried intelligence about missions and strategies.

After the war, communication was still a priority. In 1952 President Truman formed the NSA. The NSA breaks secret codes used by other nations and terrorists. It also makes secret codes to keep US data safe.

The NSA is often combined with the Central Security Service (CSS). The CSS includes the US Army, Navy, Air Force, Marine Corps, and Coast

Public Information

Some people think the CIA has many spies and secret operations. There are some secret spy missions. But there is another side to the CIA: public information. The CIA collects and distributes large amounts of information to the public. This information is found in libraries and on the Internet. One of the CIA's most popular books is *The World Factbook*. It has information about countries around the world. The CIA also publishes many maps.

National Cryptologic Museum

The NSA has a museum for its work with secret codes. It is next to the NSA Headquarters at the Fort Meade, Maryland, army base. The museum gets about 50,000 visitors per year. It is the only public museum that is part of the intelligence community and run by a government security agency. The museum shows code-breaking successes and failures. It also houses a library for academic studies.

Guard code-making and code-breaking divisions.

What Does the NSA Do?

In recent years, the NSA has collected data from radio and TV broadcasts. It has done wiretaps on phones and cell phones. The NSA has monitored e-mails, websites, and Web searches. It has recorded bank transfers, collected travel records, and monitored credit card transactions.

The NSA's mission is to use the data it collects to find and prevent terrorist attacks in the United States and around the world.

The Deputy Director of the NSA, John C. Inglis, explained what the NSA's mission is. He said:

> The United States, of course, has many organizations conducting intelligence. Sometimes those distinctions are based on the discipline that's brought to bear, whether it's human intelligence or imagery intelligence or, in our case, signals intelligence, and sometimes those distinctions are based upon the domain within which that intelligence work takes place. NSA, of course, is a signals intelligence organization; we conduct intelligence by looking for the communications of our adversaries. The second, and very important, distinction is that NSA is a foreign intelligence organization. The intelligence that we are authorized to collect, and that we report on, is intelligence that bears on foreign adversaries, foreign threats, more often than not, located therefore in foreign domains.
>
> Source: "NSA/CSS Core Values." NSA. NSA, January 10, 2013. Web. Accessed September 17, 2014.

What's the Big Idea?

Take a close look at this speech. What is Inglis's main point about what the NSA does? Pick out two details he uses to make this point. What can you tell about conducting intelligence investigations from this speech?

CHAPTER THREE

Security Agencies

O n September 11, 2001, the United States suffered the deadliest terrorist attack in its history. A terrorist group took control of four airplanes. They flew two of the planes into the Twin Towers of the World Trade Center. These were two skyscrapers in New York City. The terrorists crashed another plane into the Pentagon, the headquarters of the US military located

Almost 3,000 people were killed and thousands more were injured in the September 11, 2001, terrorist attacks.

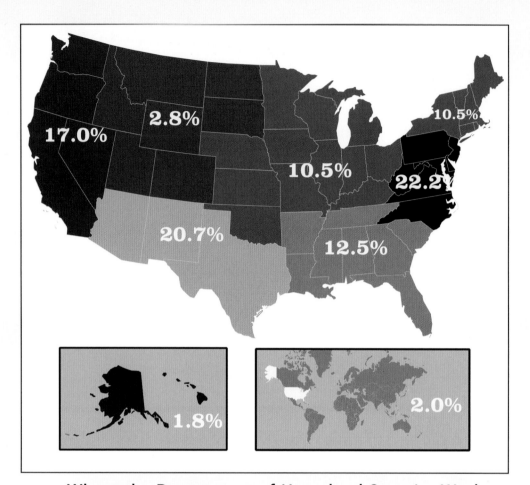

Where the Department of Homeland Security Works

The DHS is headquartered in Washington, DC. But it has offices across the country and around the world. This map shows the location of DHS employees by region. Look at the map, and think about the location of DHS employees. Why do you think there are more employees in some parts of the country? Write 200 words explaining your reasoning.

in Washington, DC. The fourth plane crashed in a Pennsylvania field before the terrorists could reach another target in Washington, DC.

In peacetime, the US Coast Guard is part of the DHS. In wartime, it becomes part of the Department of Defense.

Eleven days after the attacks, President George W. Bush made Tom Ridge the director of the Office of Homeland Security. This agency began planning how to prevent future terror attacks. In 2002, the DHS was formed. A total of 22 government security agencies came together to form the DHS. This made it easier for them to share resources, information, and staff.

US Coast Guard

The US Coast Guard provides security along the coasts of the United States. It performs sea rescues and law-enforcement duties. In 2003 President George W. Bush made the US Coast Guard part of the DHS. If war is declared, or if Congress or the president so declares, control of the Coast Guard transfers to the Department of Defense as part of the US Navy. The US Coast Guard has been a part of every major US conflict since 1790.

The security agencies work to keep the United States safe from acts of terror. They also protect against threats that come from inside the United States or from other parts of the world.

Border Security

The DHS protects US borders. It monitors all points of entry into the country. The agency screens every person who enters the United States. It also inspects all goods shipped into the country. This is done to make sure the goods do not contain illegal substances.

Border security is just one of the DHS's jobs. The DHS also helps people prepare for emergencies.

One of the Secret Service's duties is to provide protection for national leaders and their families.

These may be manmade accidents, such as a train wreck. Or they may be natural disasters, such as a flood. The DHS needs data from many sources to do its job well. It has its own intelligence network. But it also shares data with the CIA and NSA.

Transportation Security Administration

About 1.8 million people fly from US airports each day. These people go through security screening by the Transportation Security Administration (TSA), which is part of the DHS. The screening may involve passing through a scanner or a metal detector. It can also include X-raying bags and belongings. The TSA works to prevent airplane hijackings and make air travel safer.

Secret Service

The Secret Service is part of the DHS. It provides protection for the president, vice president, and other important people, such as foreign leaders who visit the United States. The Secret Service does more than just protect leaders. It also investigates crimes. The Secret Service was formed in 1865 to stop people from making fake US money. Today it also investigates banking and computer fraud.

Tough Critics

Not all people value the DHS's work. Critics think the agency wastes money and resources. Others believe it is too large to do its job well. Some people have negative experiences with DHS agencies. For example, people who travel on airplanes must be checked by Transportation Security Administration (TSA) agents. Many travelers have been delayed due to long lines at these checks. People often feel that the TSA's methods are an invasion of privacy.

EXPLORE ONLINE

The website below has more information about the Secret Service and its role in protecting the nation. As you know, every source is different. Reread Chapter Three of this book. What are the similarities between Chapter Three and the information you found on the website? Are there any differences? How do the two sources present information differently?

Inside the Secret Service
www.mycorelibrary.com/security-agencies

CHAPTER FOUR

Law Enforcement Agencies

On July 26, 1908, Attorney General Charles J. Bonaparte formed a group of special agents to work as investigators for the Justice Department. In 1932 the group became known as the United States Bureau of Investigation. In 1935 the group's name was changed to the Federal Bureau of Investigation.

Police officers and FBI agents sometimes work side by side on local crime scenes.

The War on Crime

The role of the FBI in law enforcement has changed over the years. In the 1930s, criminals terrorized the nation with robberies, kidnappings, and murders. The FBI sent agents into the field to find and arrest these people. The agents worked in dangerous conditions. They investigated criminals and worked undercover to gather evidence. Some agents and many criminals were killed in gunfights. Some of the most famous people brought to justice by the FBI include John Dillinger, "Baby Face" Nelson, Kate "Ma" Barker, and George "Machine Gun" Kelly.

Federal Bureau of Investigation

The FBI is part of the Department of Justice. It gathers facts and solves crimes. The FBI works on cases that concern threats to national security. It works with many other agencies in the United States and around the world. The FBI has law-enforcement duties. But it is not a police force. The FBI often works with state and local police forces to resolve certain types of crimes. But it only does so by request or if the crime also falls into their area of concern.

The FBI's job is to protect and defend the United States against threats that come from both within the country and around the world. It does this by working with other intelligence, investigative, and law enforcement agencies.

History of the FBI

At first the FBI only worked on banking, business, and fraud cases. During World War I (1914–1918), the FBI dealt with acts of spying, people who tried to avoid the draft, and acts of sabotage in the United States. After the war, the FBI began working on crimes that crossed state lines. This is when a crime involves more than one state. It can be unclear as to which state should work on the case. For example, a bank robber may steal from banks in more than one state. The FBI can step in to help.

During a period of time known as Prohibition (1920–1933), people were banned from importing, making, and selling alcohol. Alcohol did not disappear, though. People still made and sold it. But

During Prohibition, agents would stop and check cars for alcohol.

now they were doing it illegally. The FBI worked as a national law enforcement agency to break up crime rings involved in the alcohol trade.

The FBI continued its national law enforcement role during the civil rights movement of the 1960s. It served as the lead agency for enforcing federal civil rights laws. Today the agency still investigates and stops crimes committed against people because of their race.

The FBI expanded its reach to international crimes, such as terrorism, in the 1980s. As the Internet became widespread in the late 1990s, the FBI took on cybercrime and computer threats.

After September 11, 2001, the FBI became one of the main agencies working to stop terrorism. The FBI helps find and arrest terrorists both within the United States and around the world.

The FBI is still active in preventing and investigating crimes. But it now spends much of its

Most Wanted

The FBI has a famous list called the Ten Most Wanted Fugitives. Criminals on the list are usually very dangerous or the worst offenders. They are only removed from the list once they are captured or dead. At one time, this list was displayed in all post offices. Today the list is rarely put on display. The main place to find it is on the FBI's website. The FBI also has lists for the Most Wanted Terrorists and Cyber's Most Wanted. The FBI's website also has postings for kidnappings and missing persons.

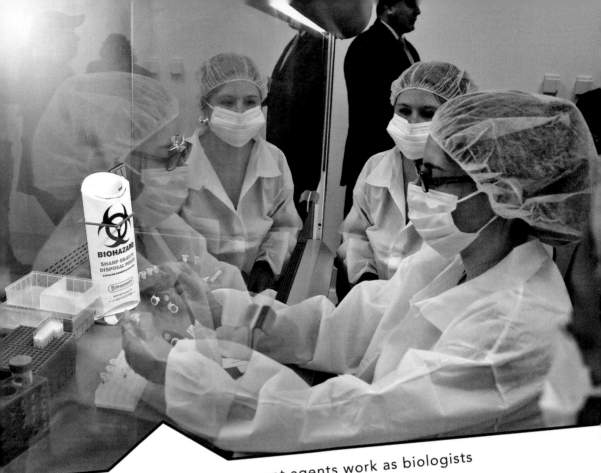

Some law enforcement agents work as biologists or chemists.

time stopping acts of terrorism. It is the lead agency for counterterrorism.

Roles and Responsibilities

The FBI employs people with a broad range of skills, training, and experience. Its many highly trained agents work on a wide variety of crimes. For example, FBI scientists work in forensics and DNA testing.

Computer specialists track cybercriminals and find hackers. Accountants review financial records, looking for crimes involving money.

The FBI headquarters is in Washington, DC. But the agency has 56 field offices in major cities across the United States. There also are smaller offices across the country and around the world.

FURTHER EVIDENCE

Chapter Four covers the FBI and its role in investigating and solving crimes. The FBI uses many techniques to perform these jobs. What methods does the FBI use to investigate crimes? Who performs investigations? Visit the website below to learn more about how FBI agents conduct investigations. Choose a quote from the website that relates to this chapter. Write a few sentences explaining how the quote you found relates to this chapter.

How We Investigate
www.mycorelibrary.com/security-agencies

CHAPTER FIVE

Interactions with the Government

Each of the security agencies has a unique role in providing protection to the United States. But they work together to reach this goal. The legislative and executive branches of the government use the data gathered by intelligence agencies to help make decisions about laws and national security.

The president and Congress rely on security agencies to help them make good choices about how best to protect the nation against threats.

IC Briefings

Each morning, members of the IC prepare a top-secret document called *The President's Daily Brief*. This document has information about new threats or warnings. It also has an analysis of the threats. The brief goes to the president, the Secretary of State, the Secretary of Defense, and the National Security Advisor. Congress has two main committees that get briefed twice a week on current events from the IC. They are the Senate Select Committee on Intelligence and the Permanent Select Committee on Intelligence for the House of Representatives. They receive classified information that most members of Congress do not get. In times of crisis, the IC briefs them more often.

Oversight

The CIA, NSA, DHS, and FBI are among the 17 federal agencies that belong to the Intelligence Community (IC). Oversight of these agencies prevents any one agency from gaining too much power.

The IC is part of the executive branch of the federal government. But oversight of the IC is shared by both the executive and legislative branches of the government. In the executive branch, oversight is the president's

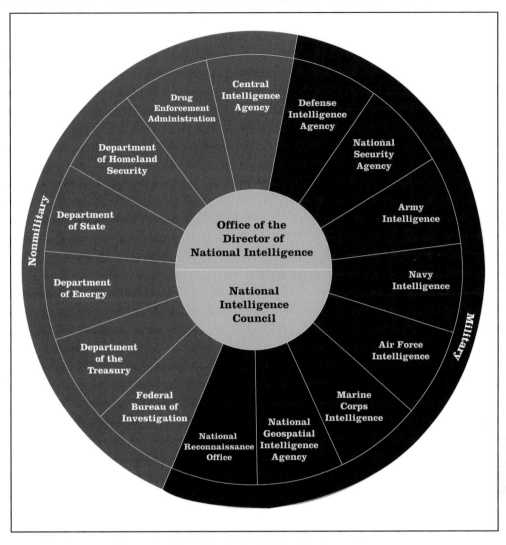

Agencies of the Intelligence Community

The Intelligence Community includes a number of executive branch agencies and organizations. Each one plays a key role in collecting and analyzing intelligence. Together they make up the complete US intelligence team. Members of the IC advise the Director of National Intelligence. How does the information in the image compare to what you have learned from the text about the IC and the agencies that are part of it? How is the information similar to what you have learned? How is it different?

High-ranking members of the IC spoke to the House Permanent Select Committee on Intelligence in 2013.

responsibility. The president relies on several committees for advice. Congress decides how much money to provide to the different IC agencies.

The executive branch decides which data Congress can access. Some of the information from the IC is top secret or classified. This means only certain people can see the information. Congress has the power to override the president's control through the use of hearings, investigations, and reports. Congress can even ask for classified information from the IC.

President George W. Bush created the Department of Homeland Security in June 2002. It was the largest change to the structure of the US government since 1947. Tom Ridge, the first director of the DHS, explained how funding of the DHS compared to other departments:

> *The new Department of Homeland Security would be composed of nearly 180,000 federal employees, drawn from parts or all of twenty-two units of government, including the Coast Guard, the Secret Service, elements of the Department of Justice, INS, security guards at airports, and Customs. The department would have an initial budget of $37.5 billion. Even so, it was less than the budget of the Department of Education and less than a tenth of what the Department of Defense spends in a year.*

Source: Tom Ridge and Larry Forbes. The Test of Our Times: America Under Siege . . . And How We Can Be Safe Again. *New York: Thomas Dunne Books, 2009.*

Consider Your Audience

Review this passage closely. Consider how you would adapt it for a different audience, such as your parents, your principal, or younger friends. Write a blog post conveying this same information for the new audience. How does your new approach differ from the original text and why?

IMPORTANT DATES

1908

Attorney General Charles J. Bonaparte creates a group of special agents to work as investigators for the Justice Department.

1920

Prohibition begins.

1924

The Justice Department begins collecting national fingerprint records.

1947

President Harry S. Truman creates the CIA.

1952

President Truman establishes the National Security Agency.

2001

Terrorists hijack four airplanes and attack the United States.

1932

The Justice Department's name changes to the Bureau of Investigation.

1935

The US Bureau of Investigation's name changes to the Federal Bureau of Investigation.

1942

President Franklin D. Roosevelt creates the OSS.

2002

President George W. Bush creates the Department of Homeland Security.

2003

Control of the US Coast Guard transfers to the Department of Homeland Security.

2013

Edward Snowden reveals the NSA has been collecting data on US citizens.

STOP AND THINK

Say What?

Studying US security agencies can mean learning a lot of new vocabulary. Find five words in this book that you've never heard before. Use a dictionary to find out what they mean. Then write the meanings in your own words, and use each word in a new sentence.

You Are There

In Chapter Five, the security briefings the president receives each day are explained. Imagine you are an advisor to the president and the daily brief contains information about a potential terrorist attack. There is not enough information to tell when or where the attack will happen. Write a short essay to explain how you would advise the president to proceed.

Why Do I Care?

The NSA has been accused of spying on US citizens by monitoring their phone calls and e-mails. How do you think this affects you today? Do you think this might affect you more in the future? Use your imagination!

Surprise Me

Chapter Four talks about the FBI. What are two or three facts you learned about the FBI in that chapter? Write a few sentences comparing what you thought about the FBI from books, movies, or TV shows and how the FBI was presented in this book.

GLOSSARY

analyst
a person who studies data

counterterrorism
taking actions to stop
terrorism

cybercrime
using computers to commit
crimes, such as hacking or
identity theft

forensics
using science to solve a crime

hacker
a person who gains
unauthorized access to
computer systems

hijack
to forcibly take control of a
vehicle

intelligence
secret information about
plans, activities, threats, or
possible threats

investigate
to closely study evidence

oversight
the act of supervising, or
overseeing, the actions of an
agency

sabotage
to purposely damage
something or hinder an
action

terrorist
any person who uses terror to
achieve a goal

wiretap
to secretly listen to another
person's phone conversations

LEARN MORE

Books

Doak, Robin S. *Homeland Security (Cornerstones of Freedom: Third)*. New York: Scholastic, 2011.

Hamilton, John. *The CIA (Defending the Nation)*. Minneapolis: ABDO Publishing, 2007.

Thomas, William David. *How to Become an FBI Agent*. Broomall, PA: Mason Crest, 2009.

Websites

To learn more about How the US Government Works, visit **booklinks.abdopublishing.com**. These links are routinely monitored and updated to provide the most current information available.

Visit **www.mycorelibrary.com** for free additional tools for teachers and students.

INDEX

ABOUT THE AUTHOR

Allan B. Cobb is a freelance writer living in Central Texas. When not writing, he spends his time backpacking, caving, hiking, kayaking, sailing, and traveling. Cobb has a background in biology, chemistry, and geology.